THIS IS

the v

TH

to

TO IRELAND.

with love
from Daylesford ♡
Australia!

01. 01. 2019.

Govind

GW01066126

Deva Wings Publications

Daylesford, Australia
www.devawings.com

After the Storm:
embracing a transformative life

Texts and illustrations by Arjuna Govinda 1956-

Deva Wings Publications 2018
Copyright (c) G. A. Govindamurti 2018

Also by Arjuna

Towards the Lion (spiritual memoir)
Heartbeat - CD Sacred songs

Also by Deva Wings Publications

The Language of the Heart
Becoming Whole : a psychology of Light
The Healing Hands of Love : a guide to spiritual healing
The Archangels and the Angels

All rights reserved. No part of this book may be reproduced by any process, nor stored in a retrieval system, transmitted, translated into another language, or otherwise copied except for brief passages quoted for the purpose of review, without prior written permission from the publisher.

NATIONAL
LIBRARY
OF AUSTRALIA

A catalogue record for this book is available from the National Library of Australia

Govinda, Arjuna, author.
After the Storm / Arjuna Govinda.
ISBN:978-0-9587202-8-1 (paperback)
Spiritual life.
Mind and body.
Self-realization.
Libraries Australia ID 63948864

Of Freedom
For Love

I live my life
by the kindness of others
and because of their love
I find my heart.

With deepest of thanks
to all who have helped me
find meaning and purpose
and Light and Love.

May you all be
most richly blessed.

&

with heartfelt thanks
to my beloved
Dorthe Klar

Prologue

With karma* being what it is, in general we humans seem to spend too much of life worrying about things that never need thought in the first place. We attach to things that simply come and go. When inspiration comes, I am reminded that Love and Spirit are ever-present. It is up to me to stay open to the blessings of these gifts, and to appreciate and enjoy life as I am able. The practicals get done and the Divine waits for my realisation.

After completing my first book *Towards the Lion* I was aware how much discipline was required to keep the writing clear, understandable, fair to all, honest - within balance, and so on. At the end of a lengthy process I felt an urge within me to write a novel where I might enjoy more freedom within the expression. To speak my mind with less concerns and even more honesty. Then, one day when I was mediatating, an angel gave me an impression that I write a book of poetry. It could just be a book where I expressed whatever I wished to share.

In an ideal world, to express the best I might aim for, I would continue to work on this book until the moment before my transition - back into spirit. But then, there is a joy in sharing something of these expressions with you now.

Hoping that it has something of value for you.

~ Arjuna

* karma - the law of cause and effect.

p.s. In any absence of punctuation, feel free to rest when you will. May I suggest you pick poems and pages at random.

Every mystic
who has gone beyond
the limitations of
the day-to-day
has shared
what they found
in poetic terms

Rumi suggested we:
'pass beyond knowledge
into madness'

Paramahansa Yogananda:
that we are free
when we realise
that 'life is a dream'

Sri Ramana Maharshi:
that the ultimate truth
is 'nothing more than
being in the
pristine state'

This book
aims to express
something
of what I find in
Being Human
and Becoming Whole

In seeking a deeper connection
with The One
True Love.

Index

Please note:

Where I have used the word 'God' please substitute whatever word or words that best work for you.

FOR FREEDOM

If I call it
a book of poetry
will you excuse my poor grammar?

If I call it
my little book of freedom
then I can allow myself
to express something of that
which is near to my heart

Without fear
of breaking any rules

For Freedom ...
For Spirit ...
For Love.

WORLDS

Perhaps
a lack of grammar
will disturb you

Perhaps
it may
awaken?

Thoughts, drawings, ideas

To live
in a free-flowing
world.

CONCERNS

I begin this book
with some concerns
that too many words
may disturb you.

To agitate mind
to take away peace
and the stillness
that resides
in the silence.

And so, my hope
you know how to choose
when to look
go within
or just listen.

1

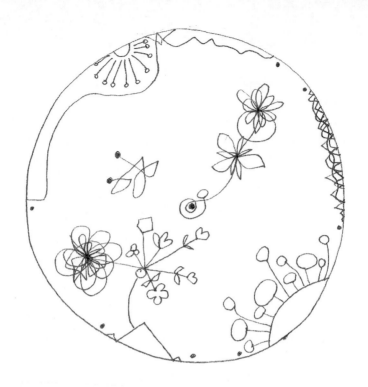

WHERE TO BEGIN?

I like myself.

It has taken a lifetime to learn
that being love in this world
includes loving myself as well.

I have been on so many journeys
Many of my choosing
many imposed because of
choices past.

Karma is perfect
the way it teaches
Complex lessons
and growth.

I seek to be honest.
The world is not all well.
Honest voices
help us to heal.

In honesty
we might find each other
in our rawness
and common humanity.

In fear
we choose pathways
other than
Love.

Love gives life
Fear steals
blessings
and abundance.

Love.
Why we exist at all.
Love, and love
and Light.

We are given paradise.
In ignorance we create hell.
Being human
there is much to learn.

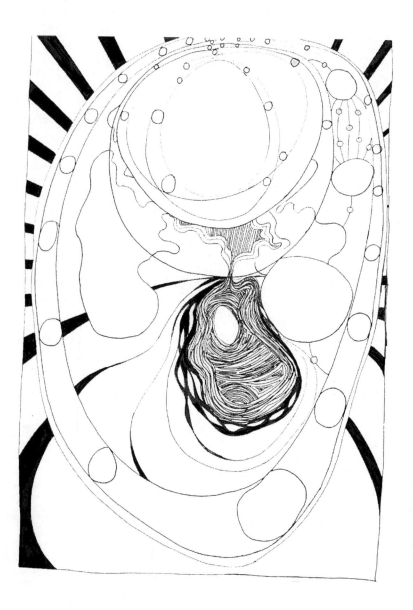

ENTERING

(our miraculous world)

A SEARCH

Every day I wake
to what I was dreaming
and take my time
to be with these inner realms.

To appreciate
what is new
of this moment
and this day.

Fortunate when I do not have to rush
or enjoying the difference when I do.

Today I wake to the dream
that I am in physical being.
Today I see I have thoughts
beliefs and senses
to inform me.

That I am but a part
of a much bigger dream.
That of Life Itself.

And each day
when the night has come
I get to rest.

In cycles of days
and seasons
and changes
each lowers or lifts me.

At night I lay myself down
and re-enter again, into sleep.
To go wherever I go
and re-enter yet again.

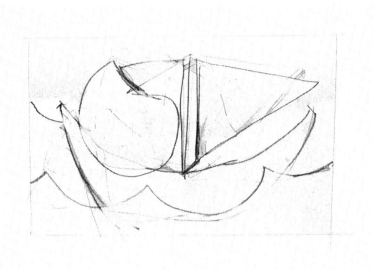

So many worlds within worlds.
Interests
expressions
and matters of the heart.

That I have found love
is such a blessing.
That I live in abundance
is also of great support.
Precious times
when I get to share with my friends.

Yet, in all of these blessings and abundance
I still search for where I belong
and what gives meaning
and purpose to this life.

TO JOURNEY

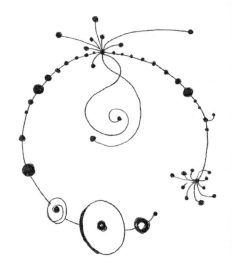

In any life
there is a time
of being called.

An inner prompting
to change how things are.

It may be as simple as
wanting something new
and it may be something
of far more consequence.

Perhaps you are content.
Or perhaps
there is a disturbance.
Some outer event
or inner sense.

You are moved
to act in some way.

An idea comes
to mind or heart
and you look
to make a change.

The hero
accepts this inner calling
to begin these
new
adventures.

And what I've learned
through making several
is to allow the fears
yet not obey.

To feel
the reluctance
to give yourself time
to be gentle but forthright
in going your own way.

WITHIN SILENCE

In silence
there may be
great peace.

In surrender
an awakening
to who I am.

In stillness
a wonder
of what might be.

In prayer
the promise
of what shall become.

ZEN

I have no idea
what to say about zen
except to share
that it helped me

To regain my health
To restore some balance
to recover the peace
when there was none

Ready to leave
a frantic world
All by itself
Zen drew my return

Beyond mind
Beyond cares
Beyond worry
A lessened pain

I quit my job and
went to the beach
Left my clothes
with the shore ...

... and began
again.

ABSTRACT

An idea comes
To write like
a painting

To express
something clear
but abstract

To place words
and sequences
of words
wherever they will ...

A symphonic
resonance

To be guided
by inspiration.
To enjoy
a sense of play

Uplifting
Awakening
Pleasant where possible

Well ...

Here we go.

NEW LANDS

I enter now, into the mystery
of this dream, within a dream
within ... who knows what

I journey, wondering, what will come
of stepping into new lands

If you come with me, I will share what I find
and the feelings that try to persuade me

A Light that beckons from the depths of my heart
I live on the edge of discovery

On pathways that lead, to spaces that invite
some courage and will, and recovery

I find a deep well, and the realm of peace
eternally present for all

Miracles we share, though taken for granted
this wonder, this mystery, in awe.

TRAVELLERS ALL

So here we are, travellers all
wandering long and with intention
Content say all, to have not yet arrived
at our final, destination

Perhaps because, we still fear death
Perhaps as well, to live?
Caught within, a great unknown
Yet to learn, to let go and give

Avoiding often, that which has value
for many a child-like attraction
Seeking here, craving there
some pleasant, but temporary, distractions

What then, before you die?
Have you found out why you're here?
To find the courage, to live your heart
And go beyond all fear.

BEYOND THE KNOWN

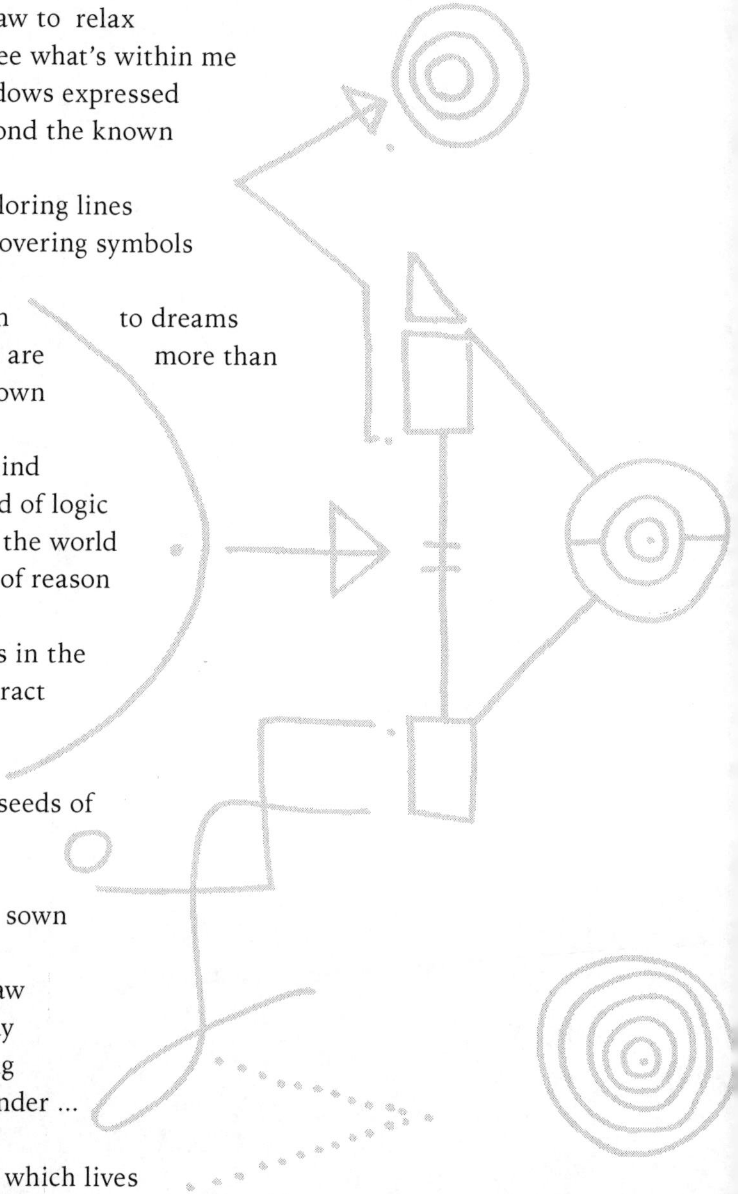

I draw to relax
to see what's within me
shadows expressed
beyond the known

Exploring lines
discovering symbols

open   to dreams
that are   more than
my own

A mind
freed of logic
and the world
full of reason

rests in the
abstract

the seeds of

love sown

I draw
I play
I sing
I ponder ...

that which lives
beyond
the known.

SOME PEACE

In this moment ...

No judgements
No projections
No concerns

Only

This moment.

HEALING

Time
in nature

Giving
to others

Opening
to higher Love

Such Grace.

BEING HUMAN

(sometimes complicated)

CHILDHOOD . DAYDREAMS

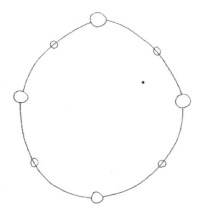

barefeet on wet grass - sunshine on my body
- warm summer days - open beach - waves -
sand castles - innocence - sunsets - the
love of family - learning to swim - sitting
on my bike - talking with friends - meeting
new people - collecting cans - glass bottle
shapes - exploring hidden alley ways -
swapping stories - collecting bubble-gum
cards - flavoured ice treats - discovering
new insects - reading love poetry - playing
war - exotic dreams - holidays - staying
up late - Christmas Eve - Christmas Day
- the promise of summer - a tortoise -
a platypus in the wild - weekends with
grandparents - stories of abundance - roast
dinners - playing marbles in the soft dirt

ADULT . INNER WORK Love = Kindness.
Generosity. Giving. Sharing. Trust.
Sensitivity. Helpfulness. Honesty. Calm.

... Becoming more whole

- autumn leaves - bush dancing - love from a distance - first inklings of romance - holding hands - first love - first kiss - going to the movies - finding treasure - the kindness of neighbours - schoolyard friends - painting lessons - first three guitar chords - fascination with rocks - rare stones - varieties of music - listening to Beethoven - the freedom of weekends - bowling alleys - high diving - hours watching lawn bowls - playing on the Monkey bars - trying out the high jump - rockpools on the beach - the wind in my hair - getting lost in big cities - camping - sitting by a river - sound of water over rocks - lizards - the smell of flowers - jonquils, roses, bluebells - paper bark trees - playing in the sand dunes - car drives on treasure hunts - cherry tree blossoms releasing their petals - forest adventures - going to the drive-in movies - pinball machines - days out with friends - walking on ocean beaches - the music of Melanie Safka, Cat Stevens, Elton John, Pete Seger, Janis Joplin - practising martial arts - licence to drive - annual meetings with old school friends - mateship - studying drama - working in theatre - finding a wider world - going walkabout ...

Fear = Anger. Trepidation. Doubt. Anxiety. Greed. Guilt. Hopelessness. Blame. Shame. Worry. Depression.

... Integrating shadow into Light

LUMINESCENT LOVER

In childhood, awakenings
together, at play
Schoolyard fantasies
perfect days

Seeing in another
a radiant jewel
Doing my utmost
to appear super-cool

First holding of hands
heart, all there is
Soft as rose petals
sharing a kiss

Open to be happy
in heaven awhile
Such treasures found
in another person's smile.

SPRING

Soon Spring
and the beauty
of flowers.

LOVING

When life was most difficult
you were always there
Facing my darkest trials
you guided me

In school I longed to meet you
to live with you in my dreams
but you were always just out of reach
and I, in other worlds it seemed

But my dream remained but a dream
and sadly, many times more
As I sought for you in fantasy
and of course, true love is much more

I found you eventually in friendships
in passion, in kindness, and in play
I found you in giving service
and the start of each new day

I find you now in blessed peace
open to where you flow
enjoying the grace of meeting you
and a harvest
so patiently sown.

21

OM, SHANTI, OM

I dream …
I am atop, a giant, ocean wave
About to be dropped, from a great height
Relaxing, I trust
I will be okay

I dream
that my partner
wants to leave me
I ask her to wait
to give me time
to prepare

I wake to hear
an inner voice

I am one with the Sun
At one with the Light
At one with all that is

I AM
life itself

I wake
to a normal
day.

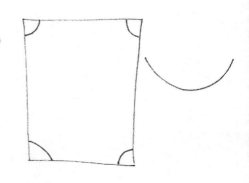

22

TO MY DEAREST
YOUNG SELF

Once I lamented
that you suffered so
a world so rigid
that stifled your flow.

Beaten most days
at school, in strife
simply for showing
your love for life.

Those who tried
to ed-u-cate you
those disturbed
by your spirited play.

How many pains
you suffered, and constant
how many times
you had to obey.

Older and wiser
now you are seeing
the potentials of peace
in your own inner being.

Rest yourself now
surrender past gall
that healing may come
to each and us all.

Come back to the fun
don't be so coy
and find new ways
to open to joy.

Find yourself now
in loving acceptance
Let go the past hurts
Take refuge in love.

A LETTER HOME, 1979

Dear all,

Everything seems
so far away
I work constantly hard
on many and varied planes

Did Amanda call
or has she disappeared?
We last met as friends
I am pleased to say

Relaxing all Sunday
two nights without sleep
Life reveals herself
and I give all
that I can

School has labelled me
idealistic
for being unrealistic
calling them to ban
using the strap
on children

An insanity among my
co-workers
many with differing views
of how to keep life at bay

I spoke with a crow
about staying away
and wore work's frustration
when I surfaced again

The weather is magical
with cloud transformations
ocean walks and pink sunsets
a break from automation

I feel like I am thirteen again
dreaming of flying

And with work and study
and parties and friends
Life is full

I currently hold hopes
of leaving the madness
and becoming
a painter
or busker
or such.

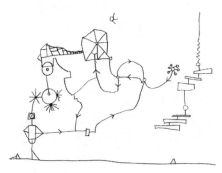

LETTER FROM NEPAL

The people here are very
serene
All is quiet, clear and at ease

We work, serve tea or cook

Sit by the fire and talk

Gather in the courtyard in
rain

Considering what neeeds to
be done
or just doing it

It gets done

The meals taste earthy
Energy circles and builds

Sometimes we are separated
then together again
United, quietly or gently
in various configurations

Within and around us
movements of calm
Some excitement
clarity and warmth

Dutch apple-pie
with soft cream from a yak
and cinnamon that tastes
direct from the earth

Some of the people eat rice
with every meal
and they feel like air
when I meet with them

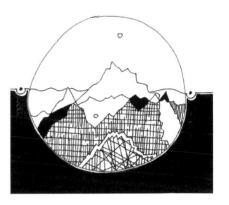

Others have an air of earth
Serene and
happy to be

We've lost or gained
time again
and I've no concern
which way

Treating myself like a king
I breath in
the mountain air.

AFTER SHE DIED, 1999

I suffer the pains of sadness and loss
that life demands of me now
To empty me of ambition
to challenge me to grow.

I willingly yield.

I open myself
to whatever is required
More than anything else
I live to serve.

Going within
to feel what is happening
And why I am here
alone.

Alone but for spirit
and angels who comfort
Alone but for nature
embracing me whole.

I feel the love
of Cosmic Mother
Immobile, grieving
another day gone.

Alone with God
a sacred sentence
These parts of me
that yearn to cry

These parts of me
that miss her
playful
Radiant spirit.

Meditating, I contact
the centre of meaning
Amidst these feelings
that weep and rage.

A constant question
that drives me near madness
Is this change to bless
or to break me?

The Light is with me
I strive to rise
Torn by the challenge
that demands
I find essence.

With every step
with all I can give
I move towards
the centre.

I give as I must
my life to prayer
and surrender
exhausted

but in trust.

WHAT TO FORGIVE?

Incessant mind
clinging to hurts
What to do
but let go?

Mirrors of self
caught in a storm
finding the truth
uneasy born.

I do what I can
to feel rain fall
to dance when able
to respect life, all.

To retrieve what is mine
to let the rest pass
I struggle, but love
to find my
true path.

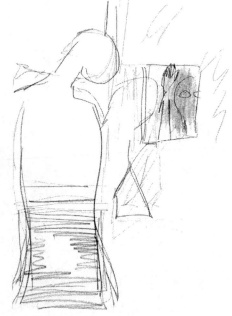

WHOLENESS

Beneath the surface
of troubles and struggle
I Am free

Beyond the illusion
of what is difficult and less so
I Am a part of all this

Deep and dark
sometimes uncomfortable
Yet, I Am whole

This part of me
that seeks connection
with All That Is

I do my best
and invoke
This Light.

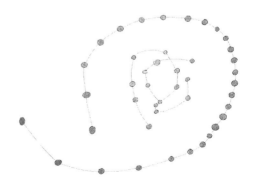

SHOULDS

"You should ..."
"We should ..."
"I should ..."

When to get a life?

"You can ..."
"We may ..."
"I will ..."
"I am ..."

Freedom
but one choice away.

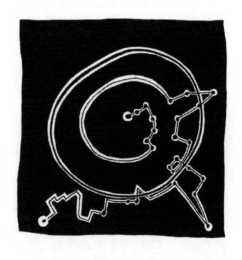

NEED TO BIRTH

Ceasing now
to strive for normalcy
for whatever it is
that feigns nature true

Seeking instead
the child within me
a need to play
and savour the new

Moving, hoping
I steer my choices
always towards
the greater goal.

THE STREAM

Poetry, childhood
teenage years
Troubles and joys
challenges, fears

Ageing, but caring
the death of a dream
waking to spirit
and play in the stream

We live, we become ...
when tired, we rest
To sleep and awake
and seek what is best

So many are starving
so many refused
oppressed, and ignored
seeking refuge

We hope for something
to come to the fore
we yearn and we crave
and still we want more

Sometimes achieving
often are tired
disturbed and left empty
by rampant desires

And whatever the reason
I am free, at this time
to enjoy many blessings
of rhythm and rhyme

Happy or sad
with challenge or pain
I open my heart
again and again

No matter how down
or out, or exhausted
I continue my journey
into this great Love.

DIARY ENTRY, 2015

I ask myself
as gently as able
Who am I? and
what do I want?

Like a zen koan
the questions force me
to go to the place
where the answer is known

Finding my questions
I relax as I ask
and fall into sleep.

I dream of a gatekeeper
who asks me a question
that people in general
would not know

In answering the question
I am given permission
to go through
to the next stage.

I ask: Who am I?

I wonder ...
Can I surrender all
to Life?
Then I might know.

If I disengage completely
from this jagged, busy world
perhaps then
I may know -
who I am
and what I want

. . .

If I can just let go of all
that I have been doing
that has kept me from
knowing
then perhaps
some clarity will come.

Rather than by adding
more ideas
that obviously haven't
engaged me

Then perhaps
in the very state
of just being
I may finally know
the truth.

To know who I am
which includes
just being
Beyond thinking.

When I paint images
without thinking
When I immerse myself
in nature
I become
in greater connection
to Who I am.

Often I find myself
when I am with others
In being with them
I am just myself

Myself in relation
to what is happening
And there is pleasure
in that

Not so much me
but more of
Us.

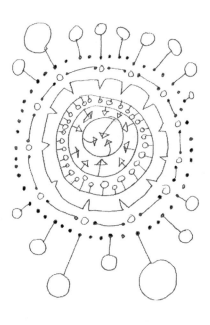

There is enjoyment
in relatedness
Of being in
Relationship

At times
doing something
Simply
within action

Feeling purpose in serving
the good of all.
I give myself space
to simply be free

I give myself time
to be away from
the thoughts
of what I think
I should be doing

And in just being ...
I feel truth

In just being ...
I feel a sacredness

In just being ...
I have no need

to understand

anything.

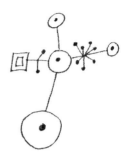

FACING FEARS

What will
become
of me
if I
cease to be?

Then I
won't have to
worry about
being me

Perhaps even
see
what is truly
Just
me

Facing
these
fears
I Am
pleasantly

Free.

SPIRIT

Many fear death
but what do we know of it?

We live
but what of immortality?

Focusing only on the physical
emphasises limitation

Where Spirit is alive
to All That Is.

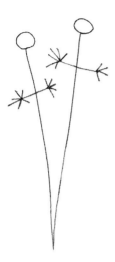

BREAKTHROUGH

Embedded within me
is life, born from love
Returned, to this heart
A messenger dove

At the end of my days
I can say with all truth
I have loved, and been loved
Richly blessed.

FRAGILE

How precious is life
when we feel it
so fragile.

THE SMALLEST DROPLET

A droplet of water
flew through the air
released from the one
Great Waterfall

It lived without cares
with fun and adventure
Mattering not
Where its life may go

It thought it was separate
and felt quite alone
But when gravity called
It fell back to its home

From whence it had come
it finished its course
to become again part of
the One True Source.

INNER WORK

I enjoy it
when it's happening
Something other
when it's not

To the best of
my ability
Equanimity
and calm

But still a volcano
bubbles inside me
wanting to storm
and to rant and to rage

And then I stay
as present as able
in choosing the best
I can and I may.

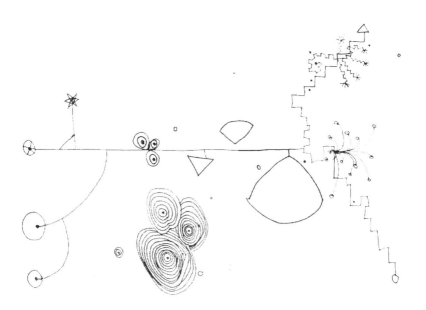

CONTEMPLATION

I am gratitude
I am endeavour
I am awe of life

I am right thinking
I am generosity
I am kindness

I am human

albeit

temporarily.

BECOMING WHOLE

In silence
In stillness
In being

Receiving
Inspiration.

Taking action
I learn

Reflecting
I integrate

Choosing well

Becoming whole.

ON THE LOOKOUT

In truth
I face the fears
that I
have
thus far

Enabled.

And accept
that there are many
more
that I am

as yet

Entertaining.

Fears of this
And fears of that
fears of fears

Everlasting.

And along the way
I do my best
to temper
such

Undermining

Emasculation.

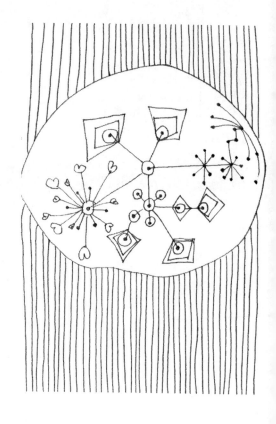

OF LIFE

God, Life, ...
What matter what you call it?
How could you not
appreciate
this
exceptional
event?

We exist
We search
We learn
We grow

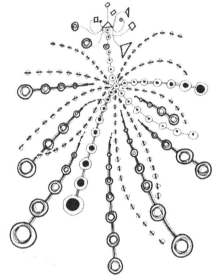

Fall in love
Lose love
Find love
All a part of
the larger gift.

Sitting quietly
Aware of peace
Aware of conflict
An innate grace

Conscious, unconscious
do you ever consider
What is most important?

Perhaps ...
to open more

To Life?

ZAZEN & RICE

Life among flowers
naked with the Sun
each morning a prayer
invoking the One.

Months without company
sweeping stone paths
pruning old branches
a storm's aftermath.

Thunder and hail
I walk in the rain
night time presses
aloneness and pain.

Most days withdrawn
a poet in zen
cherry tree blossoms
stir me again.

TILOS, GREECE

Sitting here
on this island beach …
Too few options.

To be, to wait
until I feel
to act …

To act
and then to rest.

Too few options.

EGO MIND

Contrast and conflict …
but not for me.
I am the ego
and think that I need
to be
at the centre.

I do my utmost
to maintain and resist
Who I think I am
thinks
that it needs to
persist.

I defend and I go
to all sorts of effort
to keep myself
strong, and safe
and
separate.

Yet
how does it serve me
or any one else

if I remain closed
self-focused
and
disconnect.

When I sit
and relax
and learn
how to be

I find myself
peaceful
and happy
and free.

So many lessons
in the way of
ambition

Yet …

Am I not
much more
than what
I think
I am?

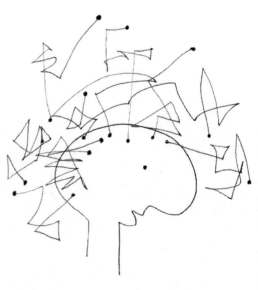

46

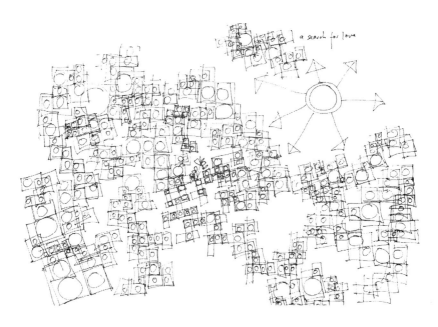

a search for love

BY NATURE'S LAW

Some are lost
Unconscious
Surviving

Wayward, distracted
hopeful, conniving

Some hurt themselves
and others
Not knowing

How or why
to allow life
in growing

Some so stressed
incessantly striving
constant and willful
but never arriving

Where then
a balance?
When then
a thriving?

Perhaps best to rest
in the arms of Creator

Love always finds us
when we are ready
to savour.

DEAR FRIEND

I hardly know you
but I feel love for you
Looking into your eyes
Watching you drift away
Come back in awhile.

So quiet in front of me
I'm healed by your smile
Watching you dreaming
Seeing you, softly
Taking time

Child of a loving God
finding your way in this world
Take the time it takes
to find what you're looking for.

You laugh and the world laughs
You smile and the world is happy
You cry, and the angels
they cry too.

And when the storm is over
you find yourself dancing
in the Light
Nothing to worry you
Dancing in all your joy
Freedom has found you now
dear friend

And life is beautiful
beautiful just like you
A treasure of the Holy One
Dear friend.

LOVE & FEAR

Allowing the fears
=   loss of life experience

Opening to love
=   generosity
=   kindness
=   fun
=   joy
=   play
=   helpfulness
=   caring
=   belonging
=   union
=   smiles
=   happiness
=   pleasure
=   confidence
=   cosyness
=   upliftment, and more.

Decision
=   when possible, remember to love.

TO BE WHOLE

Stories you tell yourself - that keep you in that story
But who are you - in Truth?
In all aspects of your - true being
Light and dark - and everything in between.

FRUSTRATION

What to write
about being frustrated?

Oh ...

It has passed.

BUSY

Busy, busy
Going to work
Busy, busy
Keeping self small
Busy being safe
Busy updating
Busy ...
Too late
Gone

A FLOATING LEAF

So many dreams
left the heart still, broken
What then becomes
my immediate task?

Like a floating leaf

Surrender
the way.

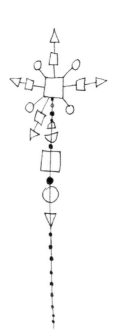

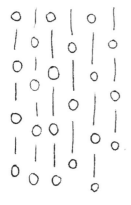

NOW

The sound of the rain
is so beautiful.

Gentle, nurturing
giving me company.

Autumn, almost passed.

The coolness invites
an appreciation for change.

Today
I am free.

AN INNER HEALING

Rising from the darkness
to stand again in Light
battles past, eternal now
'tis time to stop the fight.

Some meaning comes, so many mistakes
the times I fought to be free
how many lifetimes to face oneself
and find the courage to be.

Edges seen, and lands explored
bad days becoming years
Called to enter the furthest places
to face my deepest fears.

Lost within an intriguing madness
aware that I had finally drowned
seeing light above the chaos
in welcome grace, new life allowed.

Challenges constant, sometimes gentle
owning now my darker side ...
Putting wayward thoughts to paper
to see some where, and get some why.

Unfinished business with old foes
reliving battles, longtime passed
Inner demons now revealed
far too many but freed at last.

Ever ready for a fight
creating wars an art
willing now, to go beyond
and settle in the heart.

For peace in all
and peace in me
Alive in trusting
A life set free.

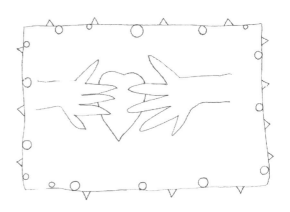

HISTORY

We assassinated Gandhi
for seeking independence
and Martin Luthor King Jnr
for similarly speaking freedom

We hanged Al-Hallaj
for declaring he was realised
and crucified Jesus
for bringing us Love

I hope you are fine
that I look at life honestly
and express when I must
some spirit of joy.

WAYWARD MIND

In play
a busyness
like a child, little care

What it thinks of as real
when quite
unaware

It claims itself king
in worlds born apart

Let go of the mind
and enter
your heart.

GOING HOME

I came to Earth
to find myself again.
To seek the Light

To reconnect
with my heart
and the Divine

To meet old friends
to make new ones

To understand
to learn
what I can
of compassion
and caring
and kindness

To see the cruelty
as we each
still learn
to go beyond our fears

So many distractions
so many paths
that take a long way around
away from the Light

This dream
within a dream
within a dream

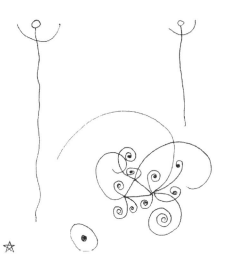

This play we each perform
Each of us
learning from the roles given
each of us learning
in our own way

Choices
Consequences
Causes and effects

We struggle
we strive
each holding onto
particular beliefs

And at times blessed
realising quietude
and stillness
Understanding
Peace

. . .

55

A joy rises
from within my heart
flooding the spirit
moving me to tears

Unexpected joys
welcome delights
simple pleasures

The occasional grand awakening ...

No more books for a time
I take a needed break
from structured learning

I come from the Mystery.
I make my way
back home.

Love calls
and I respond to that
which is
my true Self.

CELEBRATING YOU

What is not to love
about you?
A rhetorical question.

You are loved
You are wonderful

You have always been
unique and perfect
in your imperfection.

We all are.

A living creation
formed by Grace
and our own
independent
choices.

Eventually ...
each of us realise
what we are
looking for.

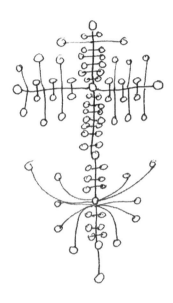

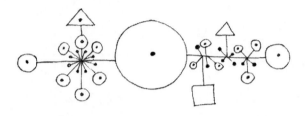

US

In stillness
I feel peace

In silence
there is us

Within
the eternal

Forever
my love.

AWAKENING TO SPIRIT

(life begins anew)

SEEKING PEACE

At times
I feel fury
As able
I let go

Recognising that
I am
Ultimately
free.

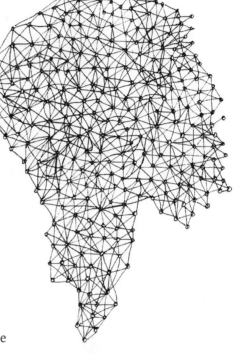

SOME FREEDOM

Acknowledging, I see
Accepting, I let go
Allowing, I release
the torrential pain.

Appreciating, I receive
In surrender, I open
In trust, I am
free again.

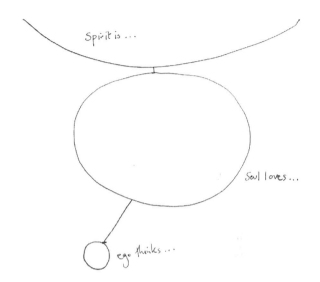

~ I ~

I think
that I am

I worry
I lose

I open
I realise

I am
That
I Am !

MORE LOVE

So I write
and I draw
and I meet you
where there is Light.

I see past darkness
as it begins to fall
Away from where
I used to shelter it.

My task
to discriminate
and share
what is in my heart.

To look to helping
and creating
more love
in this world.

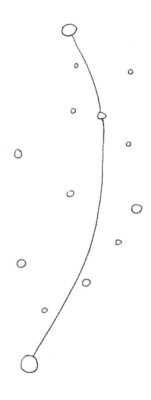

A MOMENT

What delight appreciation brings
What gifts in consciousness of being
What peace in gratitude and joy
Allowing life to flow

Awakening
Thankful
Choosing Love.

WITH NATURE

Today I am free
to be with my thoughts
To feel
the potential of being.

AWAKENING

Waking
I give myself time
to feel
and come into being

Thoughts present
and I begin to sense
movement in the muscles
A rested body
aware of my breath

I am alive
I am on Earth.

I call to Spirit
Give thanks for the day

Awaken me
to higher purpose
Awaken me
to love.

to my sacred and holy
potentials

I invite Great Spirit
into my heart
mind and body

I will to serve
To engage with life
As best
and as balanced
as able

I invite
higher consciousness
to stir
and to fill me.

A natural process.

Spirit awakens
in me

I wish to live fully
I seek to align   . . .

and again

I come alive.

REFLECTING

This day I woke to life as a dream
eternal life
within me

And then my mind
became aware
of itself
a separate entity

Seeking truth
beyond beliefs
to find what is real
for me

I live in that place
where life is joy
and spirit
forever free.

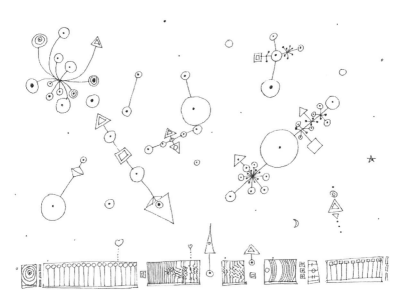

BEING

I cannot help but
wonder . . .
Is there anything
I can give to this world

Other than

To act on inspiration
when
it may come

And other than this
other than
doing what feels right
at the time

To breathe
To wonder ...

I see life all around me
I see how - I think I am
I breathe ...
I wonder ...

Endowed with Being.

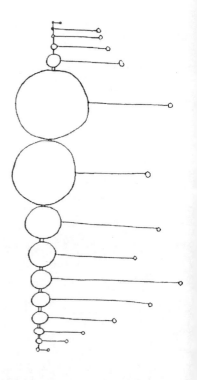

ALMOST PEACE

I seek to make peace
with myself
and all

Accepting that I am
already
what I hope to be

All I need.
All I have.
What I am.

I smile
remembering
yet again …

I am whole
I am alive
I am conscious

What more could anyone desire?

LETTING GO - THIS DREAM PLAY

I find happiness
when ceasing
to want happiness

In being
as well as becoming.

Happiness is present
in being present.

In the flow of being
experiencing what is.

In letting go of craving.

I exist in a world that is
not an accident
but a gift.

A gift that we, as humans
have the ability to make
into a paradise
or into a hell.

The creation of our choice.

I rest in the knowing
that I can sit in silence.

To simply be
and wonder
at what I am a part of.

I can sit and do nothing
unless
I feel otherwise called.

I can choose
how I think
and when to move.

Being in this present moment
I allow the mind to rest.

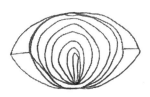

I am at peace in knowing
that everything is balanced
in its own way

and present
for its own reasons.

In this moment
there is nothing
that I actually need to do
or need to create.

In this present moment
everything that is happening
in the world
is continuing to happen
whether I like it or not.

Things that delight me,
as well as things that do not.

I seek to act in a way
that does honour
to what I comprehend
as Grace.

I seek to act in a way
that feels right for me
to do.

I act in a way
that feels
enlivening
affirming
creative
Where I can feel
my heart.

When I feel to sit quietly
then that is my action.

In sitting quietly
and doing nothing
my mind still presents me
with many thoughts.

And yet -
in doing nothing
am I not also giving?

To the well-being
of life on Earth
by giving
to my own well-being?

In doing no harm
in being one
conscious element
of this great organism
that is
essentially
Love.

I am
at peace.

I seek
to free myself
of being trapped
in the great Illusion.

To go beyond
what I have been told to believe in
and find
some actual truth.

This Great Mystery
that allows me to know It
little by little
as It calls me.

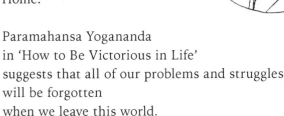

My journey
Home.

Paramahansa Yogananda
in 'How to Be Victorious in Life'
suggests that all of our problems and struggles
will be forgotten
when we leave this world.

Offering, that we
do not take this life
too seriously.
That we

'Look behind the drama
to the Master of this Universe
the Author of this dream play.'

CONSCIOUS

It helps me to write
what goes through my mind
to draw random inklings
of that which runs wild.

Sometimes in silence
sometimes quite bright
to bring what is hidden
into the Light.

To welcome emotions
I would rather deny
And give them release
a little at a time.

Could there ever be wars
if we were all more open?
To share our truths
of commonly held fears.

We could each help the other
to manage our daemons
to meet in a peace
of union so dear.

Where all agree
to let go of disturbance
And build this world
For the good-of-all.

THE GIFT

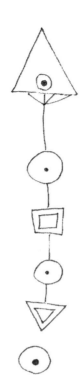

We think
we pray
we hope

We struggle
we worry
we strive

We love
and fear
to lose that love

believing
we have to
survive.

Life
Such a
puzzle.

AWAKE !

Today
I do something different
to what I did yesterday

Today
is precious.

IN PAINTING

I paint some pictures to cope with life.
In painting, I feel free to express.

I have no training except in the creative process
but I can draw
and I can put paint to paper
or to canvas.

In painting I am free.

In painting, I sit quietly
and explore feeling.

What images want to be created.
What lives still
in the unconscious realm.

I allow myself
to explore
what is.

Some days it feels like life itself.
Other days
my mind wants to get involved.
Pushing me
as to what to paint
or how.

Mostly it is a process
of just being with the impulses
that emerge from allowing
the space for that.

In painting I can feel myself active

In a fun way.

Unlike school
where there were often many rules
And rule givers.

Prompting me ...
What to do ...
How to do it ...
Why and wherefore...

Now
by myself
it is a wondrous
and relaxing time.

I surround myself
with paint and brushes

77

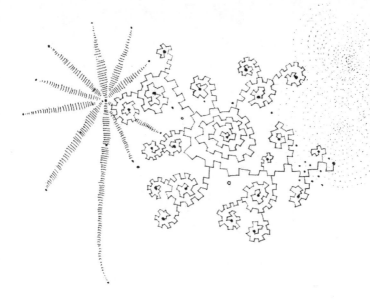

and other objects
for applying the paint.

Then …
Simply observing
what happens!

Painting becomes a process
that is important to me.

When I am painting
and feel 'not at peace'
I continue anyway.

If I don't like the image
or how it is going
then I just remind myself
that the Process isn't
Yet complete.

Do I feel done with it?
Does it feel done with me?

Any chance to be free
from a demanding mind.

In painting
I can be with myself.
I can be with being.
I can be with what
The process has
to show me.

Sometimes -
what it may teach.

In any case
it feels freeing and healing.
The opportunity to explore

Something
without restrictions.

And in painting
I like to approach it
in the way
I would like to approach it
once I know it better.

To paint with full courage

and without attachment.

So those qualities
need to be part of my
expression
right now.

Learning to trust
the intuition

Being open to hear
some guidance within.

Perhaps an example
of learning

to be human

and free

and whole.

I DRAW A CIRCLE

I draw a circle
and wait

As something stirs
within me.

I delight to see
what unfolds

Of this random
but pleasant
creation.

What comes to be
from some simple lines

What worlds present
as I draw and observe

A smile !

SEEKING UNITY

What is my duty
but to find myself?

What can I do for you
but to be true to me?

As an artist
I strive to share
the spirit I feel
the beauty I see.

Inspired
I find fulfilment -
in sharing some thoughts
with you.

Listening
I hear the wind.
Feeling
I find us together.

Beloved
Will you help me?
To find this unity
in all.

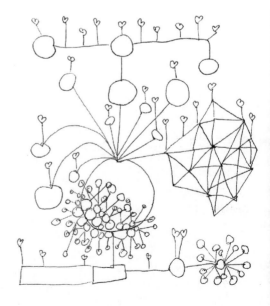

ALIVE

Alive
I wake
to feel
An opening

Intuition
to guide me.

I open
to Spirit
for inspiration

I find
The courage
to be.

With wisdom
With balance
In awe

Connecting
with who I am

I train myself
to be content
and grateful

To allow
the fullness
of life.

Radiant with love
I become
This holy grail.

THAT WHICH ABIDES

Watching my body
I age
Being with soul
I am free

Best, I think
to focus on
That which abides
in Thee.

CIRCLE

We gather and connect
Go within and share

A choice to be present
and honest and care

We meet and we speak
responding to a call

Being who we are
for the benefit
of all.

MY 40TH YEAR, 1996

In my 40th year
I worked with the principles

Love, Acceptance, Choice & Will.

It was the foundation
of a very good decade.

LOOKING TO THE STARS

Looking to the stars
I find a sense of belonging.
Comfort, peace and
a sense of perspective.

Contemplating the Divine
I wonder
if our very first gift is freedom.

Freedom to be
Freedom to choose
Freedom to awaken

To ever-greater consciousness
and Love.

And life becomes
what we choose to do
with such
magnificient blessings.

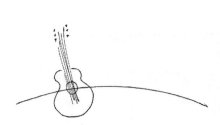

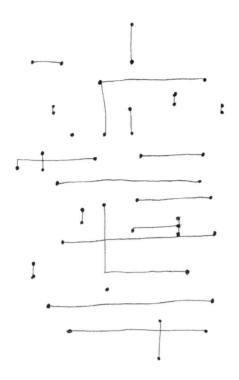

LEGACY

What legacy will I leave this Earth?
What might I create with my time?
The idea of a perfect circle

In giving, in creating, in being

To love life
To acknowledge its blessed gifts
To be true.

KNIGHT'S CHOICE

I do my all
to go beyond
this nagging ego.

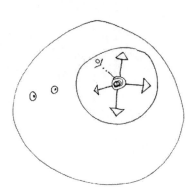

IS THAT SO ?

Say what you like
about me
Everything is fine
I know that my choices
are always
to Love.

MAZE

He learned the secret, of a complex maze
No longer feared restriction
In a contrast world, he survived the threats
and dreams of near extinction.

Confident, there would always be
safe passage on his way
An aging man, but now confirmed
to be present for his stay.

He found the place, beyond his fears
of human limitation
and in that knowing, a confidence
to work for liberation.

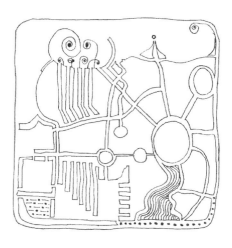

BECOMING CONSCIOUS

I am surrounded by images
and symbols -
Stories being told
and retold -
Then it comes to me ...
I have been dreaming.

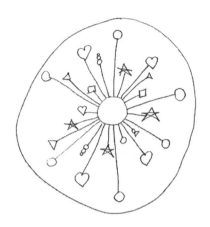

I can see how my mind
is going over details -
Dreams as they try
to show me things.
Stories told in symbols
that my psyche
may somehow
Come back into balance.

That the complexities of my experience
might be clarified
and Resolved
again.

My body feels stiff
and some soreness from lack of exercise.
I am happy to be alive again
and to contemplate the possibilities
of the new day.

Today there is nothing pressing.
I get to come into life slowly -
The way I enjoy it -

and savour
Being conscious.

Some days, I would rather
just stay in bed
but today
I have things to do.

Today there are
adventures.

Adventures
To be lived.

SOME DAYS ...

Some days dizzy
Some days lost
I draw a circle
to calm me

Some days surprises
like today in style
some times confusion
left wondering why

I draw my circles
and fill them in
happy to see
whatever they give

No agendas
No expectations
just a brief respite
from an active mind.

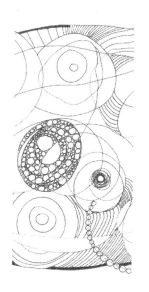

PREPARING TO DANCE

Preparing to dance
I stand
first, my body.

Getting a sense
of being
Here, now.

Drawing in spirit
I open to consciousness
Feeling a breath
as it enters my lungs.

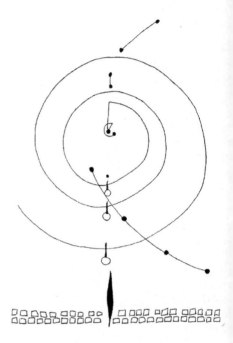

Called to move
steadied by Presence
sounds of a singer
that touches my heart.

Feet bare
soft earth
Inviting the feelings
to enter and flow.
An expressing of joy
while feeling the grief
So many worlds
are waking and converging.

A universe within
a desert without.
This quiet inner place
I enter, and move.

The dancer feels
the Dreamtime comes.

Free again
in sacred space.

Problems past
I express myself
Aware of contrasts
that make for the play.

The dancer awakens
as I feel drawn to move
to surrender myself
in Spirit again.

For love and for life
In prayer and in awe

To balance -
To find harmony -

In Cosmos
once more.

NEVER ALONE

This beach extends for many a mile
yet I have it all to myself.
Barefoot, without time to press me
I stroll along the sand.

In a rock pool near the water's edge
a crab goes about its business.
My gaze upon this tiny creature
Calls its senses to mine.

Two long metres between our eyes
it cannot possibly see me
yet aware of my attention
focused upon its being.

Gazing skyward, I am also aware
beyond my physical vision
another consciousness, higher still
Makes its presence known.

Immediately obvious
I live in the middle
of at least
three different worlds.

Never alone.

INFINITE

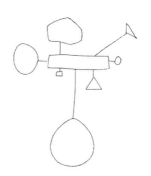

How little is known
Of All That Is.
How rarely we ponder
Life's fullness.

To think, just a moment
To close our eyes.
To feel our lives
such a miracle.

How much is unknown
is, of course, unknown
except, this divine-spun
illusion.

In going within
the blackest of black
an endless space
In infinity.

The eternal nature
and essence of things
Now I wonder
is all a reflection.

All that we seem
and more, beyond that
So vast what we are
both outside and in.

SO MANY WAYS

How many ways to live this life?
What choices do I make?

Why so many questions
on what I'm doing here?

What can I do?
What might I give?
What are my sacred gifts?
How often do I manage
to connect myself with that
which feels important?

Do I care?
Do I dream?
Do I seek?
Do I give?

Which season is my favourite?
What memories enrich my life?

Do I make the most of the time I have
before I have to leave?

Is it in my heart to cry?
Is it in my heart to laugh?

So many ways to find the hidden treasure.

:)

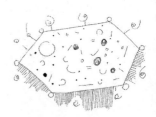

PLACE OF DREAMS

What might I call this place
but Grace
that I am able to be
So peaceful.

Drawn into a tapestry
of tiny sounds
Small birds merge
with the warming Sun.

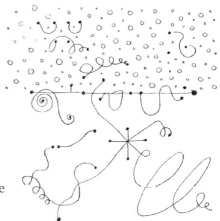

Silently, quietly
a smile presents on my face
as I am taken into
this other space.

From the peace of simple pleasures
to a hint of inner bliss.

Almost to tears
the inner realm
greets me now.

Familiar and friendly.
The One
Loving Kindness.

Full, having just eaten
Resting on a wicker chair
I surrender into this loving
intimate

Place of dreams.

DREAMING

What matter
if I feel this force
coming from
inner worlds?

What comes to us
through us
that seeks
to bless.

Such Love
beyond being human
It fills us
finding home.

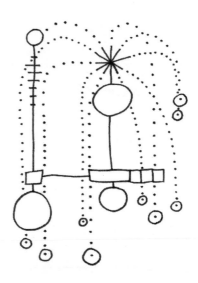

TRUST

I learn to love
through letting go.

I learn to trust
what is.

DISCOVERING THE PATH

(life with purpose)

BEYOND THIS DREAM

Seemingly real
but somehow impermanent
In truth so brief
beyond this dream

What might we find
look past the drama
What might be given
if we sought the Author

To go within
to find some answers
The truth is there
for the pilgrim sincere

The longer around
the more we are guided
The more revealed
of a sacred place

But attach too much
to the pleasures of this world
then the more pain also
when it's time to leave

Let us give -
to Life
Let us go -
to Love.

SO MANY RICHES

Once I had nothing
and everyday
I wandered

Unwell
poor
but happy

Now abundant
most days
in gratitude

Inner wealth
Loving kindness
Blessed friends.

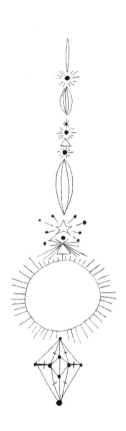

PEACE WITHIN

Busy mind
Peace within
Eternal now
and ever-present.

Contrast has purpose
conflict, a gift
Structures, how
we learn and grow.

More peace in awareness
in understanding and practice
Becoming more conscious
each time I give.

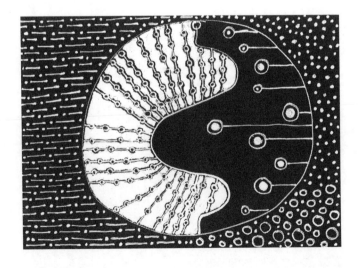

OPPORTUNITY

We are all but a thought
in the mind of God
Unknowing players
in a Cosmic Dream

Hurt and wanting
yearning to heal
An inner life hidden
but one day revealed

What say you now
that you are older
Do you live your passion
or chase away dreams

Do you hear your own heart
or follow another's
Each day closer
to the bliss in truth.

BRIDGE

Crossing the bridge
from self to selfless
can be a struggle
without zeal.

Letting go
finds ego pains
and open wounds
to heal.

But when the work
is mostly done
new worlds
begin to open

Such ease arrives
in willingness
when mind is
finally coping.

Through broken heart
and lessons learned
the Love Divine
pours in.

Bridge

ABANDON ALL

Joy comes
in giving
in yielding
and play
the love
of life present
to give
The way.

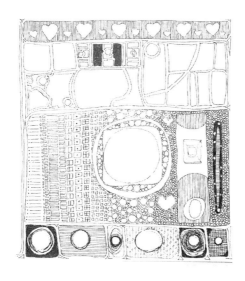

WARRIOR OF LIGHT: STAND TALL

Born at midnight, he has yet to find himself
to fully align with
his sacred path

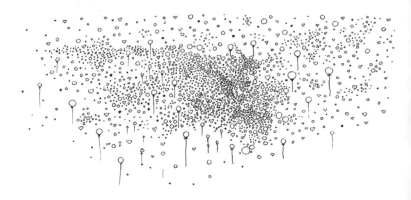

Presented with the statement
"Man choose ...
... light or dark. Man choose."

He is taken aback
He resists the relevance
thinking he is already in the light

This inner voice gently insisting
"Man choose ...
... light or dark. Man choose"

He makes his choice
and learns that it is okay for him
to have boundaries.

He responds, sensing
a higher call

Wounded in previous battles
he had given up the fight
to changing winds

Prompted now
to be of greater service
to be a clearer voice
in a fragmented world

The time had come
to establish firmly
to raise himself
from a buried past

To face his shadow
and emerge victorious
to live
a sacred potential

A beacon of light
a haven for peace
The time had come
to embody true nature

Doing whatever he needs
to heal himself

Conscious and unconscious
wanted and unwanted
He works to embody the
whole

Integrating, balancing
taking action
To be a warrior of Light

The potential of Love
the joy of his soul
the light of Spirit
'Arjuna! come!'

He learns to love
he accepts the pain
He comes to allow
his heart to weep.

He acknowledges the time
it takes to heal
He practices the wisdom
as best he may

He treads the longer journey
Slowly
Patiently
and with appropriate
caution

He walks the way of the
heart.

AWAKE

The fish
thinks itself

to be
nothing more
than a fish

when in truth
it is part of

the water
its life
depends on

and the air
that infuses

and the gravity
that holds

and the movement
of celestial bodies

All One.

PILGRIM OF ETERNITY

Life
within

Life
without

Life
Everlasting . . .

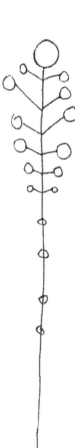

IN THIS MOMENT

Though troubled so often
by a mind busy doing
when silence descends
I am humbled again.

SHARING

A question that is constant
how best to serve this world?
What gifts to share in wisdom?
What actions, best unfurled?

I seek to find the divine
to develop what I am
a humble work in progress
this Spirit, now as man.

All my unknown nature
all efforts not in vain
as I approach the Holy Grail
Light shines upon my pain.

Shadow aspects of my being,
the heavy readies flight
as I awaken to the hidden
that craves the healing Light.

Through working on my lower self
redeeming what I can
ever closer to the more
the holy that I AM.

So best for me to help this world
to make an effort right
to do my work, to best myself
through serving first, the Light.

OPEN MIND

A mind that knows the answer
and surrenders what it wants
to allow itself to quieten
if only, long enough.

That the ever higher nature
may be heard, amidst the low
that the busyness of worldly ways
unfinished, finds a flow.

Unattached to any outcome
In peace, becomes this mind
Silent ... at least sometimes
To let the god-self shine.

THIS LOVE

The deeper I go
in opening to peace
The closer I feel
This Love.

HOPE

To act when clear
To enjoy one's aliveness
To seek inner guidance
in difficult times.

To open to Spirit
To serve the Plan
To live in the moment
In trust, I am.

TO BE & TO DO ...

There are only two things to do in life

1.   to be receptive to the Divine &
2.   to become That Love.

DESCENDING

I surrender all
to find
my true self

Descending …
from mind
into being.

MOVEMENT & CHANGE

How could I think
there could only be good times?
Am I caught in that
illusion again?

When life needs movement
a river needs flow
and I to embrace
all change.

The ego grieves
for what it thinks lost
but soul calls me inwards
and spirit draws me forth.

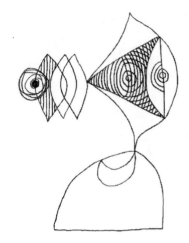

THINGS I OBSERVE

Thoughts that serve me
thoughts that wound me
thoughts that have
their own way.

I see them arrive
ganging together
too often surprised
how they trick me again.

So many thoughts
creating lost stories
so much activity
this lower mind, mine.

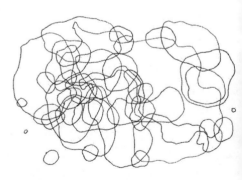

MENTAL PEACE

Step 01 – Think only thoughts that make you feel good.

Step 02 – Don't even think about Step 02 until you have practised Step 01.

Step 03 – Never lose your sense of humour.

Step 04 – Think only thoughts that open you to Life.

MORE OPTIONS

Rationalise
until the cows come home

Or -

Sit
Wait
Wonder . . .

Inspired
Act
Review.

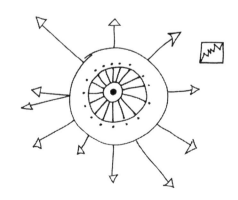

I AM LOVED

I place my trust
that Life
will support me.
Whether it raises or lowers
I know I am loved.

Though it crushes
my attachments
though it calls me to grow
still ... I know love is present -
I am loved.

In trust, I can open
In trust, I rejoin
In trust, I submit
to ever more blessings.

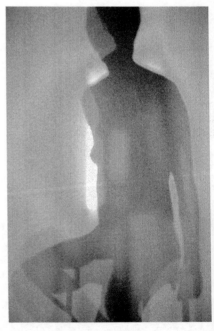

In trust, I affirm
Love is present
Love is present.

All is well
All is well
All is well.

BELIEVING

This
or something better
will always be my experience.

CHECKLIST
THINGS I THINK I KNOW

. We are part of a vast and incredibly complex creation and exist because of a myriad of specific circumstances.

. It is advantageous to health to be relaxed and present, conscious and happy, calm and at peace.

. We are all an aspect of All That Is.

. At one with That which creates, sustains and eventually re-assimilates us.

. We return, back into Its Being - when this life is done.

. Within vast complexities of being - we have choice and our choices have effects.

. It is advantageous to health to be honest with oneself about what you feel and what you choose.

. Being human includes experiences we enjoy and prefer - as well as those that are beyond our control.

. Perhaps best accepted
for what it is - walk
a path of least resistance.
Heart and will.

. In all, life is experienced
more richly when we can
acknowledge and accept
what is - and what happens
to us.

. Placing my trust in life
brings me a greater sense of
peace - and enjoyment of it.

. Worrying seems to simply
create disturbance.

. It is possible, that all I
see and experience, are but
a mirror of what is inside
me - the culmination of
past choices - to be worked
through or to be let go
of. This idea helps me to
disengage from some, more
painful, inner torments.

. Sooner or later my physical
body will return to the earth.
And my spirit will live on.

. In the meantime, I live by
the mantra - Surrender and
will. Surrender to Spirit and
use will when inspired.

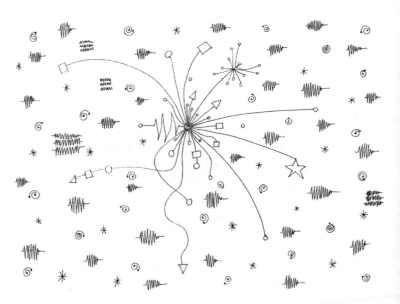

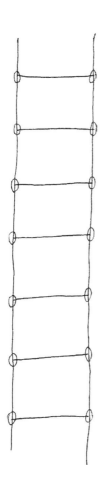

I AM

I am the masterpiece
of my own choices.

Here
now
always.

Truth
Goodwill
Loving Kindness
Harmlessness
Dharma
Dedication
Awareness
Liberation

FIVE REMINDERS

1. Find a way to **Relax**. - It will be in peace where I will receive insights and true understanding.

2. Practice living in a state of **Trust**. - That which has created me - also sustains me. Trust allows greater flow of life - and when it is time for me to leave this world for the next - how better to enhance the transition - but to trust?

3. As often as possible, find a way to **Appreciate** life - the way it is. To be in a state of non-resistance to life - and in an appreciation of it. In this state of appreciation - I am more able receive life's gift fully.

4. Whenever possible, be aligned to **Love**. - By love is life - and in service to life - I am most alive. In **service** to Love - I feel the Divine.

5. And - as each of these four already do - acknowledge and experience that I am a part of a Greater Whole - and **Merge** with That.

As best as able
I go beyond fear
and savour
all that life offers.

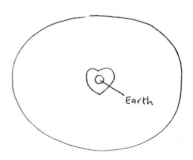

SURRENDER TO MAJESTY

(return to the One)

THE BLESSINGS OF SILENCE

In silence we may find
the Presence
of the Source of All

PLAY

And what is freedom
but a letting go
An allowing of life
to permeate.

And what is spirit
but standing tall
Responding to challenges
big or small.

A measured accepting
of all that is
becoming receptive
to life's sacred tune.

In all creating
to exercise choice
embracing life's gifts
wanted or not.

At the end of the day
to be comforted sure
in trusting and sensing
Majesty.

I do what I can
to tread the way
to become the kindness
that counts not the cost.

Grateful, these years
in my practice of love
as I learn to befriend
this heart of mine.

NOTE TO SELF

Surrender to
the higher Will.
As known
When possible.

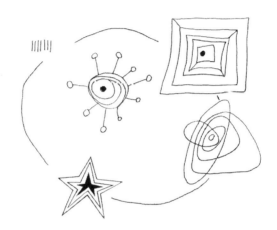

TRUE PURPOSE

My essence is joy
My purpose, play
My mission, creative
awakenings.

May you ever find
and celebrate often
the fullness of who
you are.

ONLY IN STILLNESS

Only in stillness,
do I find
what I was looking for.

MATH

Surrender + Trust = Miracles
I open to Unconditional Love.

ALWAYS HOPE

The smile of a young child
awakens me.
What shall I create
with this new-found joy?

When and how
will we learn
To be more kind
To let go of fear.

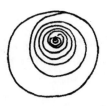

So much suffering and conflict
yet today, there is hope
and I open to be that
in this most blessed world.

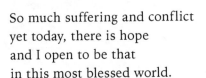

HUMANNESS

Sleepy
Dreaming
Awake
Arrived ...

Abundant
Playful
Inspired
Alive ...

Human
Complexity
Spirit
Abounds ...

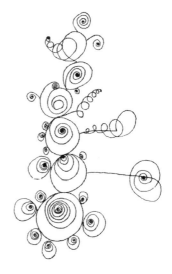

Heartfelt
Generosity
Kindness
Surrounds ...

Humble
Loyal
Hopeful
Held dear ...

Devoted
Courageous

The naturalness
of tears.

SITTING

Not doing, I rest
Resting, I contemplate
Contemplating, I am moved
An Inner knowing.

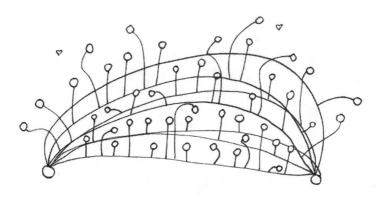

CLOSE

Aware, I smile
content, and at peace
Free of concerns
I breathe.

Entertaining
this moment
with gratitude
and awe

I am peace
I am joy
I am love itself.

Dear God
release me.

ALLOWING CONNECTION

Not by what I have
but in what I am able
to live without.

By love is life.

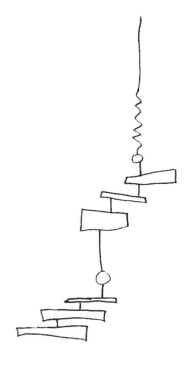

REALISATION ...

In stillness
At peace.

A quiet
realisation.

PEACE WITHIN

What is essential?
What is important?
What is potential?
What is right now?

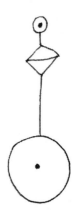

A MOMENT IN PRAYER

I Am Spirit in action
Heart in practice
The love of life itself.

I am the essential
smile.

Encompassing all
This wonder-filled
Moment.

Arrest me
Into
Your loving embrace.

Ha!

WAITING

Patiently sitting
amidst the confusion
gentle conflicts
that came with the fall.

All that exists
in order to teach me
I go within –
hoping for more.

Nearing the top
of this
holy mountain
Nearing the end
of a journey sublime

To finally find
what I spent my life
searching
A sanctuary of quiet
and sense of divine.

In Peace
in Love
in Bliss

Truth at last.

WITH YOU

To Spirit, I open
In soul, I surrender
Playing, I find you
My dear, blessed friend.

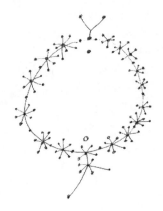

BLISS

Aware of Thee . . .
Free from all earthly desires
Thy Joy.

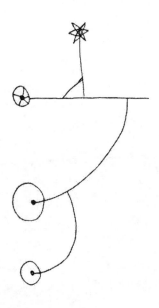

RE-AWAKENING

(aligning to love)

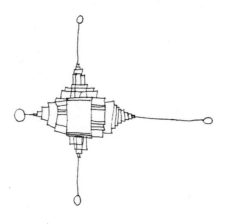

SOON

Giving over to God
I meet my beloved.
Surrendering will
I am alive again.

Life allows me to strain
and wrestle with thinking
but responds to my heart
when the time comes right.

So many years
I struggled in exile
but such a gift
to re-enter the Mystery.

INTO THE FIRE

Love has found us
Willing - and hopeful
Joyous ...
Alive again.

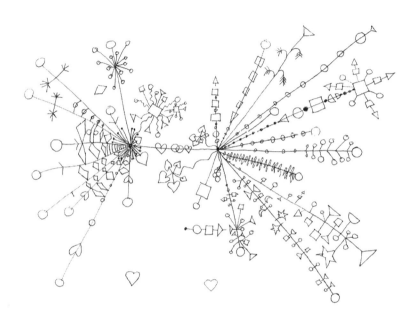

My heart bursts open
In gratitude, and wonder
This Love ...
Awakens me to Joy.

Into the mysteries
Into the wonder
Into the love of life
Into the garden

My love you are
All that I hoped for
You take me in
Into your heart

Early on we chose
Not to contain this
But to allow it
To run its own course

. . .

I feel each of us on fire
Burning in the oneness
My heart calls me to be
All that I am

For this new life
For the wonder
For the Love
that is Here for all

Into This Heart
Into This Fire
Into the Presence
Of Love Divine

My love you are
All that I hoped for
You take me in
Into your heart

Where each of us finds solace
and joy within the other
A sacred inspiration
Bringing us peace.

Love has found us
Willing - and hopeful
Joyous
Alive again.

In this sanctuary
I find myself - with you
This garden so profound
Within our hearts

And so I surrender
And so I surrender
Into this love with you
Into the Fire.

And I surrender
Into this love with you
Into the burning flame
Into the Fire.

And so, I surrender.

SAYING YES

Every day
less sleep
Every moment
closer to God.

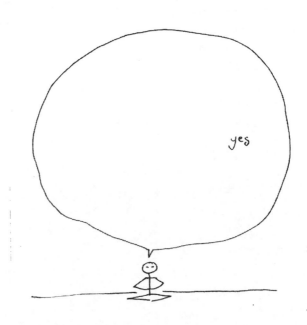

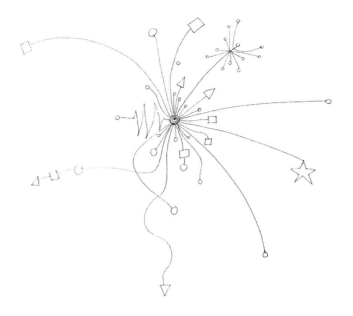

ALL ELSE FLOWS

Taking time out
at a Buddhist ashram
I feel an inner guidance.

Be open and willing
A compassionate heart
Hold all in love, as they heal.

Be there.
Be present.
Be a vehicle of love
in their pain.

That
and nothing else
is required.

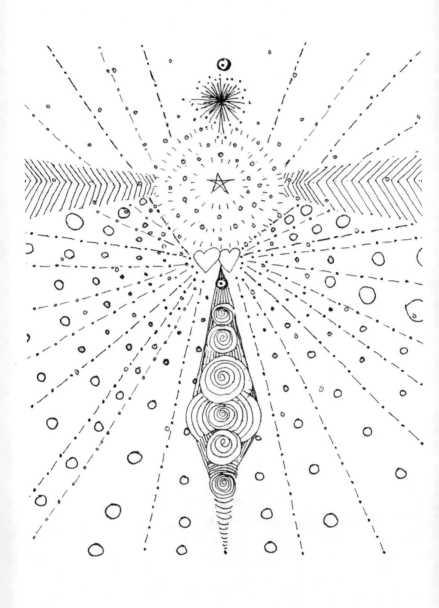

SAT – CHIT – ANANDA

I am an artist
in love with God
a student of this
Great Mystery.

In awe of the stars
and the vast
potentials
born in my heart.

I open now
to whatever Life
calls from me.

To know
This Grace
ever more deeply.

To feel This Love
even more profoundly.
This spark of light
this passion now.

I can call life a success
because I acknowledge my Creator
and express the fullness
of what I am.

Whatever I may become
I live to know God's Love
and give near constant thanks
that I find my way
back Home.

Into my Father-Mother's
Infinite Love.

I bow to That
which gives me

Being
and Consciousness
and Bliss.

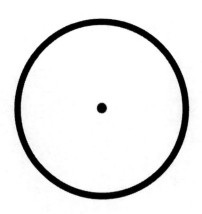

THE LONGER I LIVE

The longer I live
the more I wonder
if surrender to Love
is the only goal.

The Divine that created
and now sustains me
also welcomes
my love for all.

The more I surrender
the more I feel
closer to That
most Glorious One.

Life has brought me
into this world
patiently waiting
my inevitable return.

To find, I seek first
the most important of all
To be at one
in Thy
true Grace.

I AM

Moment by moment
open to inspiration
genuine to all
I Am

Your beloved child.

ENVISION THE FUTURE

(what we create)

I am Love

Humanity awakens

The Earth is honoured and cared for.

Grace awaits.

ABOUT THE AUTHOR

For over thirty years Arjuna has worked to understand the human condition and the inner life. He has travelled widely, creating healing music, facilitating sessions in dance and creative expression as therapy, and presenting on spiritual psychology and holistic and transformational paradigms. He presently facilitates workshops focusing on Men's Health and Creative Awakenings. When not travelling, he treasures a simple life in the mineral springs town of Daylesford, Australia.

Arjuna's interests include heartfelt company, continual learning, sacred music, time in nature, community well-being, holistic psychology, eastern philosophy, cinema, world travel, gardening and Zen. He continues to enjoy and be fascinated by life.

Arjuna is also the author of a spiritual memoir - Towards the Lion and music CD - Heartbeat.

Some Literature that has inspired
and supported over many years

Early Days

The World's Love Poetry - ed. Michael Rheta Martin
The Prophet - Kahlil Gibran
Catch 22 - Joseph Heller
Reach for the Sky - Douglas Bader
Candide - Voltaire
Zorba the Greek - Nikos Kazantzakis

Awakening

I Haven't Had To Go Mad Here - Joseph Berke
The Miracle of Mindfulness - Thich Nhat Hanh
Zen Mind, Beginner's Mind - Shunryu Suzuki
Zen in the Martial Arts - Joe Hyams
Introduction to Zen Buddhism - D.T. Suzuki
The Tao Te Ching - Lao Tzu
Memories, Dreams and Reflections - C. G. Jung
Walden - Henry David Thoreau

Healing

The Bridge Across Forever - Richard Bach
Illusions - Richard Bach
Siddhartha - Hermann Hesse
The Hitchhiker's Guide to the Galaxy - Douglas Adams

Psychology

The Road Less Travelled - M. Scott Peck
Owning Your Own Shadow - Robert A. Johnson
Transformation: understanding the three levels of masculine
consciousness - Robert A. Johnson
Embracing Ourselves: the voice dialogue manual
   - Hal & Sidra Stone

Spirituality

The Art of Happiness: a handbook for living - H.H. the Dalai Lama & Howard C Cutler M.D.

Conversations with God Book 1 - Neale Donald Walsch

Chants of a Lifetime: searching for a heart of gold
  - Krishna Das

Serving Humanity - Alice A. Bailey

Ponder on This - Alice A. Bailey

Autobiography of a Yogi - Paramahansa Yogananda

The Language of the Heart: is spoken all over the world
  - Tarajyoti Govinda

By His Grace: a devotee's story - Dada Mukerjee

Man's Eternal Quest - Paramahansa Yogananda

The Divine Romance - Paramahansa Yogananda

From the Outer Court to the Inner Sanctum - Annie Besant

The Path of Discipleship - Annie Besant

The Fire of Creation - J.J. Van Der Leeuw

The Living Word of the Hierarchy - Ananda Tara Shan

Death: the Great Adventure - Alice. A Bailey

The Holy Science - Swami Sri Yukteswar

Education

Out Of Our Minds: learning to be creative - Sir Ken Robinson

The Element: how finding your passion changes everything -
Ken Robinson with Lou Aronica

Personal Help

The Work - Byron Katie

Loving What Is - Byron Katie

The Wise Heart - Jack Kornfield

Zero Limits - Joe Vitale and Dr. Ihaleakala Hew Len

How Can I Help? - Ram Dass and Paul Gorman

To Be Victorious in Life - Paramahansa Yogananda

How to be Happy All the Time - Paramahansa Yogananda

Joyful Evolution - Gordon Davidson

Art & Therapy

The Artists Way - Julia Cameron
Art is a Way of Knowing - Pat. B. Allen

Jungian Psychology

Carl Jung: wounded healer of the soul - Claire Dunne
King, Warrior, Magician, Lover : rediscovering the archetypes
of the mature masculine - R. Moore & D. Gillette
Inner Gold - Robert A. Johnson
Ecstasy: understanding the psychology of Joy
   - Robert A. Johnson
She: understanding feminine psychology - Robert A Johnson
He: understanding masculine psychology - Robert A Johnson
Living Your Unlived Life - Robert A Johnson and Jerry M Ruhl
Femininity Lost and Regained - Robert A. Johnson
Lying with the Heavenly Woman - Robert A. Johnson

Along the Way

A Thousand Names of Joy: living in harmony with the way
things are - Byron Katie
After the Ecstasy, the Laundry - Jack Kornfield
The Search for Happiness - Annie Besant
Inspired Destiny - Dr. John DeMartini
The Big Leap - Gay Hendricks
The Vortex - Ester and Jerry Hicks
Paths to God: living the Bhagavad Gita - Ram Dass
Compassion in Action: setting out on the path of service -
Ram Dass and Mirabai Bush.
Man's Search for Meaning - Victor E. Frankyl
Anam Cara : a book of celtic wisdom - John O'Donohue
Rumi Day by Day - Maryam Mafi
The Way of Passion: a celebration of Rumi - Andrew Harvey

Writing

The Writer's Journey: mythic structure for storytellers and
screenwriters - Christopher Vogler

. . . and so many more
but forgotten . . .
or yet to come my way.

Titles by Deva Wings Publications

The Language of the Heart : is spoken all over the world
    - by Tarajyoti Govinda (1991)
The Archangels and the Angels
    - by Tarajyoti Govinda (1998)
The Healing Hands of Love: a guide to spiritual healing
    - by Tarajyoti Govinda (1997)
Becoming Whole : the psychology of Light
    - by Tarajyoti Govinda (1998)
The Joy of Enlightenment
    - by Tarajyoti Govinda (1999) (eBook)
Towards the Lion
    - by Arjuna Govinda (2015)
After the Storm: embracing a transformative life
    - by Arjuna Govinda (2018)

Available Print on Demand

Other References

www.govinda-klar.com
www.musicheartjourney.com
www.innerwork4men.com

www.devawings.com

Also by Arjuna Govinda
Towards the Lion

At 23, Arjuna's health collapsed and his chosen career abruptly ended. The author saw this as an opportunity to search for insight into the human condition and connect with his true inner self. Arjuna faced various challenges and tests along the way as he sought meaning and purpose in a complex world.

Towards The Lion is the autobiographical account of one man's quest for love, light and inner peace. The author shares the unusual path his passion for learning led him on, and his mystical connection seeking joy in life. Arjuna gives an honest look at the many blessings and challenges of the spiritual path.

Deva Twings
PUBLICATIONS

30789837R00089

Made in the USA
Columbia, SC
30 October 2018